F-18 HORN[ET]

MULTI-MISSION WAR[PLANE]

F-18 HORNET
MULTI-MISSION WARPLANE

Robbie Shaw

Airlife
England

ACKNOWLEDGEMENTS

This book provides comprehensive cover of USN east coast and USMC units, for which I am indebted to Bert Byers, the Public Affairs Officer at Cecil Field, and to MCAS El Toro, Iwakuni and Beaufort, with a special thanks to Capt. Jim 'Kaiser' Wilhelm of VMFA-333. I am also indebted to the Canadian Armed Forces for the considerable assistance I received from them, and to the Spanish Air Force.

Friends and colleagues who have also contributed, include Peter Foster, Tony Holmes, Toshiki Kudo, Frank Mormillo, Duncan MacIntosh, Peter Russell-Smith, Don Spering and Andy Thomson.

Unless otherwise credited all photographs were taken by the author.

First published in the UK in 1992
by Airlife Publishing Ltd.

British Library Cataloguing in Publication Data available.

ISBN 1 85310 202 4 (Hardback)
ISBN 1 85310 203 2 (Paperback)

Printed in Singapore by the Kyodo Printing Company (Singapore) Pte Ltd.

Airlife Publishing Ltd.

101 Longden Road, Shrewsbury SY3 9EB, England.

ABBREVIATIONS

ACLS	Aircraft Carrier Landing System
AETE	Aerospace Engineering and Test Establishment
AFB	Air Force Base
CAF	Canadian Armed Forces
CAG	Commander Air Group
CFB	Canadian Forces Base
CVW	Carrier Air Wing
CVWR	Reserve Carrier Air Wing
DDI	Digital Display Indicator
FLIR	Forward Looking Infra Red
FOL	Forward Operating Location
FRS	Fleet Replacement Squadron
HAS	Hardened Aircraft Shelter
LERX	Leading Edge Extension
MAG	Marine Aircraft Group
NASA	National Aeronautics and Space Administration
NATC	Naval Air Test Center
NATO	North Atlantic Treaty Organization
NSWC	Naval Strike Weapons Center
NTPS	Naval Test Pilots Center
NWC	Naval Weapons Center
OCU	Operational Conversion Unit
PMTC	Pacific Missile Test Center
RAAF	Royal Australian Air Force
ROKAF	Republic of Korea Air Force
SAM	Surface to Air Missile
SATD	Strike Aircraft Test Directorate
US	United States
USMC	United States Marine Corps
USN	United States Navy
USNR	United States Navy Reserve
USS	United States Ship
VA	Navy Attack Squadron
VFA	Navy Strike Fighter Squadron
VMA(AW)	Marine All-Weather Attack Squadron
VMFA	Marine Fighter-Attack Squadron
VMFA(AW)	Marine All-Weather Fighter-Attack Squadron
VMFAT	Marine Fighter-Attack Training Squadron
VMGR	Marine Aerial Refuelling & Transport Squadron
VX	Air Test and Evaluation Squadron
WSO	Weapons Systems Operator

Opposite: The first operational Hornet squadron was VMFA-314 'Black Knights' which formed in August 1982, becoming operational in January 1983. Early build F/A-18A 161710 'VW-03' was photographed on a rain soaked El Toro ramp in the aftermath of a storm. *(GB Aircraft Slides)*

INTRODUCTION

The origins of the McDonnell-Douglas F/A-18 Hornet date back to the mid-1960s and the Northrop P530 Cobra lightweight fighter project, which eventually became the YF-17, and ultimately lost to the F-16 in the contest to provide the USAF with a new generation lightweight fighter. For Northrop this was a serious blow: not only did the company lose out on providing the USAF with well over 1,000 aircraft, but follow-on orders for a number of European NATO air forces planning to replace their ageing F-104 Starfighters also went to the General Dynamics product.

On the sidelines the United States Navy and Marine Corps were watching with interest. To meet their requirements Northrop teamed up with McDonnell-Douglas, a company with extensive experience designing and building carrier-borne aircraft; thus the F-18 was born. Although based on the YF-17 design, the F-18 is virtually a different aircraft, with an amazing amount of changes to the Northrop design. The internal fuel tanks and the aircraft's gross weight were doubled, and the folding wings were just the start of a number of changes required for carrier operations. The main undercarriage legs were

strengthened considerably to withstand the high sink rates of carrier landings, and the track was widened to provide greater stability for manoeuvring on a carrier deck. Tyre size was increased, and the single wheel nosewheel was replaced by a sturdier two wheel version, complete with launch bar for catapult operations and, of course, an arresting hook was fitted under the rear fuselage.

Early in 1976 the Navy announced full-scale funding for the Hornet programme, with production of eleven aircraft for the flight test programme. Two versions were planned: the F-18 air superiority fighter and the A-18 ground attack version, with a planned procurement of 1,377 aircraft for the Navy and Marine Corps. Meanwhile Northrop continued development of a lighter weight land-based F-18L variant which lacked the radar of the naval Hornet, and was aimed at foreign sales. Prior to the fall of the Shah, Iran was a potential customer for up to 250 F-18Ls. A bitter legal battle between Northrop and McDonnell-Douglas ensued, with claim and counter-claim of using each others' technology. This dispute lasted until the early 1980s. The F-18L variant in the end never materialized.

In September 1978 the prototype Hornet was rolled out at the McDonnell-Douglas St Louis factory — the same place that had spawned the famous F-4 Phantom. Two months later, on 18 November, the Hornet took to the air for the first time, accompanied by an F-4 Phantom and an F-15 Eagle as chase planes. The aircraft quickly impressed those test pilots who flew it. In March 1979 the Naval Air Test Center at Patuxent River, Maryland received its first Hornet for service trials. Within a year of its first flight the Hornet had completed initial sea trials aboard the USS *America*. Like many new aircraft the Hornet did not perform faultlessly during the test programme; amongst the problems were poor acceleration and roll rate. These were eventually cured, though a heavier and stiffer wing was required to improve the roll rate. A number of aircraft from batch one had already been delivered before the cure was found, and all but the first nine aircraft were retrofitted. During the test programme at 'Pax River' it became obvious that the Hornet was a truly multi-role aircraft, and the Navy decided that there would be no requirement to have separate F-18 and A-18 squadrons, hence the rather clumsy official designation F/A-18.

The main reasons for the Hornet's adeptness is its manoeuvrability thanks to fly-by-wire flight controls and

the Hughes AN/APG-65 multi-mode radar which is equally good in both the air – air and air – ground modes. The aircraft is powered by two General Electric F404 engines, each producing 16,000lb thrust. It has nine external hardpoints for carrying ordnance and fuel tanks. AIM-9 Sidewinder missiles can be carried on wingtip pylons, with AIM-7 Sparrows on the inboard pylons or nacelle fuselage stations. The latter position is also frequently used to carry laser designator and FLIR pods. The inboard and centreline stations can also be used to carry bombs, mines, rockets and air to surface guided weapons. An M61 20mm gun is mounted in the nose just forward of the cockpit and a retractable in-flight refuelling probe is situated on the forward starboard fuselage. The Hornet

has been cleared to operate from minus 3g to plus 8g, a remarkable achievement. A unique feature of the Hornet is the lack of dials and instruments in the cockpit, where instead three five-inch by five-inch Digital Display Indicators (DDIs) dominate. On these a wealth of information can be displayed at the touch of a button.

The first production F/A-18A was delivered in November 1980 to VX-4 at Point Mugu. Following deliveries went to VX-5 and the Naval Weapons Center at China Lake, and to VFA-125 at NAS Lemoore, the training unit for west coast squadrons, which initially trained all Marine Corps pilots also. The first operational squadron to equip with the Hornet was in fact a Marine Corps unit, VMFA-314 at El Toro in January 1983, and it was quickly followed by VMFA-531 and VMFA-323. In the USMC the Hornets replaced the F-4 Phantom. whilst in the USN it began to replace the A-7 Corsair for use aboard carriers. The first Navy squadrons to equip were VFA-113 and VFA-25 at Lemoore, both embarking with CVW-14 on the USS *Constellation* for the aircraft's first operational tour at sea. Prior to this event a Hornet had completed 'hands-off' automatic landings on board the USS *Carl Vinson* using the Automatic Carrier Landing System (ACLS). The next

Below: Armed with an AIM-9L Sidewinder missile an F/A-18C of VFA-87 is seen over the Mediterranean whilst operating with CVW-8 aboard the USS *Theodore Roosevelt.* *(Author's collection)*

squadrons to convert to the Hornet were VFA-132 and VFA-131 which, after training at Lemoore, moved to Cecil Field, the base for east coast units. VFA-106, the east coast training unit, was next to convert to the F/A-18; both training units employed a large number of two seat F/A-18Bs.

While the Americans were becoming accustomed to their new machines the first export customer, the Canadian Armed Forces, received its first aircraft in the summer of 1982 for 410 Squadron — the Operational Training Unit. The F/A-18 was chosen in preference to the F-16, one of the main reasons being the reliability of a twin engined aircraft, a very important factor when operating over the frozen wasteland of northern Canada in winter. The official Canadian designation for their machines is CF-188, though this is frequently abbreviated to CF-18. The name Hornet is not officially used by the Canadians as it does not translate to the same meaning in French. A total of 113 CF-18A and twenty-five CF18Bs were ordered, with options on a further twenty aircraft. These were to equip eight squadrons which at the time were flying the CF-5A, CF-101 and CF-104. Within a couple of years of operating the CF-18 the CAF found that their aircraft were suffering from a problem that the US operators were now aware of, fatigue near the base of the tail fins. This has since mainly been rectified; however, it did force some unit assignment re-organization, in that 409 Squadron relocated from Cold Lake to Sollingen and assigned to NATO. The final CF-18 was delivered in early 1988, by which time the total acquisition had been amended to ninety-eight CF-18As and forty CF-18Bs.

The Royal Australian Air Force was the second export customer for the Hornet, which was preferred to the F-16 for its ground attack capabilities and twin engined reliability. The Australian F/A-18 was chosen to replace the Mirage IIIO in both the air defence and air – ground roles. Fifty-seven F/A-18As and eighteen Bs were ordered to equip three squadrons and an operational conversion unit. The latter was the first recipient when two aircraft were delivered to RAAF Williamtown in May 1985, although two aircraft were delivered eight months earlier, but were retained in the USA at Lemoore for training. The first two Hornets were built by McDonnell-Douglas, but later aircraft were constructed in Australia from kits supplied by the American manufacturer and eventually complete licence-built aircraft were rolling off the Avalon production line. The final RAAF Hornet was delivered to No. 3 Squadron on 12 May 1990.

Third export customer for the Hornet was the Spanish Air Force (Ejercito del Aire) which envisaged procurement of 144 aircraft, though due to funding problems this was ultimately reduced to seventy-two. These comprise sixty EF-18As and twelve EF-18B two seaters, with local designations C.15 and CE.15. The prefix, incidentally, stands for España. The Spanish chose the Hornet for its air to ground capability, a role in which it would be primarily employed, and for its capability as an air superiority fighter to complement the existing air defence fighters the Mirage IIIEE and F1EE. The first Spanish aircraft flew on 3 March 1986, and the first twelve aircraft off the production line were the two seat EF-18Bs. These remained in the US at Whiteman AFB where the first cadre of instructors were trained. In July the first deliveries to Zaragoza took place and Ala 15 was formed. Subsequently Ala 12 was re-formed at the same base where conversion took place, prior to moving to Torrejon where the Hornets replaced F-4C Phantoms. The final Spanish aircraft was delivered in mid-1990.

Back in the USA, the F/A-18C with improved avionics first flew in September 1986 and is the version currently in production for the USN. Some units, such as VFA-25 and VFA-113, have already transitioned to the C model, relinquishing their old mounts to reserve squadrons such as VFA-203. The C model has the advantage of being able to use the AGM-65F Maverick and AIM-120 AMRAAM. The two seat variant of the C model is the F/A-18D, though a two seat all weather/night attack variant for the USMC retains the same designation, and the first unit VMFA(AW)-121 formed in early 1990. This latest version will replace the A-6 Intruder in Marine Corps service. There are plans for a further five squadrons to convert. One of these, VMFA(AW)-225, will replace the RF-4B recce Phantoms.

The Hornet has been successful in being selected by three other air arms, to replace its fleet of A-4s and Mirage F1s the Kuwait Air Force has ordered thirty-two F-18Cs and eight F-18Ds. Deliveries were due to commence in August 1991, however the Gulf War delayed things somewhat.

Opposite: Head-on shot of a VMFA-115 Hornet.

Another sale in doubt is that of thirty-four machines to the Swiss Air Force to replace its Mirage IIIS aircraft in the air defence role. The Hornet was selected by the Swiss Air Force in a 1988 fly-off competition against the F-16. However, with the ending of the Cold War, support from some politicians for scaled-down armed forces, and a devious bid from Dassault with its Mirage 2000, have put the Hornet programme in jeopardy.

An announcement from Seoul on 20 December 1989 that the Republic of Korea Air Force (ROKAF) was to receive the Hornet was met with considerable surprise. As the ROKAF already operates the F-16 it was widely anticipated that this type would be selected for licence-production in South Korea. It was not be be, however, and the ROKAF will receive 120 Hornets. The first twelve will be built by McDonnell-Douglas for delivery in 1993; the next thirty-six will be supplied in kit form for assembly by Samsung Industries, who will then build the remaining seventy-two from scratch. The mix of single and two seaters has yet to be announced.

Another possible sale was to the French Navy of about twenty or so ex-USN F/A-18As as badly needed replacements for their ageing F-8E Crusaders which operate from the carriers *Clemenceau* and *Foch*. This however could have put the Rafale programme in jeopardy, and it was no surprise to the author when the French shunned the foreign competitor and chose instead to refurbish the Crusaders.

There is no doubt that the Hornet is an exceptional aircraft which excels in both the air – air and air – ground role, and I have yet to meet a Hornet pilot who wants to fly any other type of aircraft. No disrespect to Northrop, but perhaps it was inevitable that the Hornet was going to be a success; after all, it came from the same stable as the F-4 Phantom and F-15 Eagle. By the end of 1990 almost 1,000 Hornets had been delivered and there is no doubt that the type will become a legend amongst warplanes.

(Robbie Shaw, January 1991)

Opposite: The first unit to receive any new aircraft destined for the US Navy or Marine Corps is the Naval Air Test Centre (NATC) at Patuxent River, Maryland. The NATC is divided into several different directorates, each responsible for a specific type of research. Hornets are assigned to the Strike Aircraft Test Directorate (SATD), and used to carry the tailcode '7T,' as seen on this F/A-18A. Note the cameras on the starboard wing tip pylon. *(Peter Russell-Smith)*

RESEARCH, TEST AND
TRIALS UNITS

Below: The SATD is responsible for testing all carrier-borne aircraft and their associated equipment. The first eleven pre-production Hornets produced were all earmarked for test and development flying, with the majority assigned to Pax River. Production F/A-18A 161925 wearing 'D'Skunk' logo and unusual colour scheme is assigned to SATD. *(Peter Russell-Smith)*

Opposite: Naval aircraft armament testing is undertaken by the Naval Weapons Center (NWC) at China Lake, California. The NWC is located in a barren area of southern California and is about one million acres in size. A pair of single seat Hornets are seen over part of the range complex. *(Don Spering)*

Opposite: Another component on NATC is the Naval Test Pilots School (NTPS). Like its counterpart, the Air Force Flight Test Center at Edwards AFB, the unit uses a variety of aircraft to train test pilots for US and friendly air arms. This colourful F/A-18B is one of a couple of two seat Hornets assigned. *(Peter Russell-Smith)*

Below: The SATD has changed its tailcode from '7T' to 'SD,' as seen on F/A-18A 161937 with the modex '150.' *(Peter Russell-Smith)*

Below: Most of the pre-production batch of Hornets have now been transferred to NASA's Dryden Research Center at Edwards, where they are used for chase plane duties and research into the aircraft's amazing high angle of attack capability. For these tasks the aircraft are normally painted in high visibility markings which are evident on this F/A-18B. *(Andy Thomson)*

Opposite: Based at NAS Point Mugu, California is VX-4 'Evaluators.' As the squadron nickname implies, the unit evaluates naval fighter aircraft, and therefore undertakes trials of the Hornet in its fighter role. Also based at Point Mugu is the Pacific Missile Test Center where hundreds of missiles are launched every year during naval trials. Both units operate a small number of Hornets, and VX-4 aircraft carry the 'XF' tailcode. *(Andy Thomson)*

UNITED STATES MARINE CORPS

As mentioned earlier, the first operational Hornet unit belonged to the Marine Corps, and as the Corps needed to replace its ageing Phantoms it was given priority and received the bulk of aircraft from the second and third production batches. Marine Aircraft Group (MAG) 11 at El Toro was the first to dispose of its Phantoms, and its three component squadrons, VMFA-314, 323 and 514, were Hornet equipped by the end of 1983. These were followed by the squadrons of MAG-31 at Beaufort, VMFA-115, 122, 251, 312, 333 and 451. The next unit to convert was the former Phantom training squadron, VMFAT-101 at Yuma, which transferred to El Toro. Prior to this all Marine Corps pilots were trained by the Navy. The final USMC front line Phantom units, VMFA-212, 232 and 235 of MAG-24 at Kaneohe Bay, Hawaii had converted to the Hornet by the end of 1989, these being the first USMC units to equip with the F/A-18C variant.

The 1st Marine Aircraft Wing at Iwakuni, Japan also has two F/A-18 squadrons. These however are deployed from their US bases for a six-month tour of duty, and usually comprise one squadron from Beaufort and one from El Toro/Kaneohe Bay.

The 1st Marine Reserve unit to convert from the F-4S was VMFA-134 at El Toro, which did so in 1989. The two remaining Phantom Reserve squadrons, VMFA-112 at Dallas and VMFA-321 at Andrews, will no doubt convert in the not too distant future.

From the outset the Marines wanted the two seat F-18 to replace its Phantoms, arguing that for its role it required a two crew aircraft with a WSO in the rear seat. These wishes were not granted and the Corps had to accept the single seater. Events have now turned a full circle, and VMFA(AW)-121, the first unit to receive the all-weather night interdiction variant of the F-18D, was operational by the end of 1990. A further five units are planned to equip with this variant, their A-6E Intruders being transferred to the Navy. One of these units, VMFA(AW)-225, is due to take over the reconnaissance role from VMFP-3's RF-4B Phantoms.

Left: The honour of being the first east coast unit to trade its Phantoms for Hornets in 1985 belongs to VMFA-115 'Silver Eagles' of MAG-31 at MCAS Beaufort, South Carolina. A newly re-sprayed F/A-18A sits on the squadron's flight line at Beaufort.

Opposite: When first formed the 'Silver Eagles' had a large eagle painted on the fin. Lately this has given way to a much smaller eagle inside a circle. Sadly, due to restrictions on colourful unit markings, these markings are barely visible from a distance. This aircraft was photographed on the taxiway at Beaufort.

Below: Tail markings of VMFA-115 'Silver Eagles' USMC.

Below: Despite the lack of colour VMFA-122's 'DC' tailcode and crusader shield dominate their aircrafts' tails. *(Duncan MacIntosh)*

Opposite: After training with VFA-106 at Cecil Field, VMFA-251 'Thunderbolts' joined MAG-31 at Beaufort in 1986, and another F-4 unit had succumbed to its successor. Unlike the previous Beaufort units, the squadron's thunderbolt insignia is painted in a bold shade of dark blue and unusually, the unit's 'DW' tailcode is on the inside of the tail fins.

Opposite: F/A-18A 161964 'DW-03' at rest on the Beaufort flight line. Note that the aircraft carries the '03' modex not only on the nose but also on the rudder and flaps.

Below: Tail markings of VMFA-251 'Thunderbolts' USMC.

Below: The last MAG-31 unit to convert from Phantoms to Hornets was VMFA-312 'Checkertails' who did so in 1988. The squadron has dispensed with its black and white checks, and now has toned down dark and light grey checks across the top of the fin, which surprisingly are bordered by a yellow (above) and red (below) stripe. Inside the tail fin are the words 'Fight's On.'

Opposite: The first unit to receive the F/A-18D all-weather night strike variant was VMA(AW)-121 'Green Knights,' which disposed of its A-6E Intruders and began conversion to the Hornet in late 1989, becoming VMFA(AW)-121 in the process. The El Toro based squadron is now operational, and its first aircraft is featured over the Californian desert.

Opposite: Ground crewman checks the tyres before positioning the chocks on 'DR-08' of VMFA-312.

Below: This VMFA-314 machine was photographed during its landing roll at El Toro. The unit markings are extremely subdued, with a toned down lance and knight's head on the fuselage, and no tail markings apart from the unit's 'VW' tailcode.

Opposite: An F/A-18A of VMFA-312 returns to the squadron parking area after an air combat training mission. Although Marine Corps Hornet units are employed primarily in the air to ground role in support of ground troops, they frequently practice air combat — much to the pleasure of the pilots.

Right: Tail markings of VMFA-312 'Checkertails' USMC.

Below: A VMFA-323 F/A-18A taxies past a hangar displaying the unit badges of all three MAG-11 Hornet squadrons. This photograph however was not taken at El Toro, but at Iwakuni during the 'Death Rattlers' second deployment to the Japanese base in April 1990.

Opposite: With refuelling probe extended, a VMFA-314 Hornet approaches a KC-130 tanker. The 'Black Knights' saw action when, during a cruise aboard the USS *Coral Sea*, the squadron participated in the strikes against targets in Libya. *(Frank B. Mormillo)*

Opposite: F/A-18A of VMFA-323 landing at NAS Miramar.

Below right: Tail markings of VMFA-323 'Death Rattlers' USMC.

Below left: 'Death Rattlers' Hornets share the Iwakuni ramp with OA-4M Skyhawks. VMFA-323 and sister unit VMFA-314 have both served a tour of duty on board the USS *Coral Sea*.

Below and opposite: This head-on and tail-on view of a
Hornet shows to good effect the large flaps and ailerons.

Below: VMFA-333 'Shamrocks,' also known as 'Trip Tre,' traded in its F-4S Phantoms for the F/A-18A in 1987, and is a component of MAG-31 at Beaufort. The bright green shamrocks which once adorned the Phantoms have changed to a shade of light grey.

Opposite: 'Shamrocks' Hornets framed by the nose of an aircraft from VMFA-312.

Opposite: A VMFA-333 Hornet taxies into the 'hot' refuelling pits at Beaufort. After landing USMC Hornets frequently use the 'hot' refuelling method and refuel with engines running. This saves time and often pilots can fly two missions without having to shut down and vacate the aircraft.

Below: In this close-up head-on shot the gun ports are easily visible midway between the nose radome and cockpit transparency.

Below: Terra firma! The wheels of this VMFA-333 Hornet make
contact with the Beaufort runway at the end of another training
mission. The pod on the port fuselage station is an AN/AAS-38
FLIR.

Opposite: With a 330 US gallon fuel tank on the centreline pylon,
a 'Shamrocks' Hornet taxies out for another mission.

Opposite: Plenty of smoke from the tyres as a 'Shamrocks' F/A-18A lands at Beaufort. Like many units, the squadron paints its ownership of fuel tanks, as marked on the centreline tank.

Right: Tail markings of VMFA-333 'Shamrocks' USMC.

Below left: Beaufort based VMFA-451 'Warlords' probably have the most colourful unit markings of any USMC Hornet unit. A large dark blue speedbird logo, within which are five white stars, adorns the fin. Across the spine in toned-down markings is a grey sash with dark blue stars, although on the squadron commander's aircraft this sash is dark blue with white stars.

Opposite: VMFA-451 transitioned to the Hornet from the Phantom in 1987 and, like most MAG-31 units, has since completed a deployment to northern Europe in support of NATO exercises. It also embarked with CVE-13 on board the USS *Coral Sea* for a Mediterranean cruise in 1989. One of the unit's aircraft basks in the early morning sunshine at Beaufort.

Below right: Tail markings of VMFA-451 'Warlords' USMC.

Opposite: In 1983 VMFA-531 'Grey Ghosts' traded in its tired F-4N Phantoms and converted to the F/A-18A at Lemoore. On completion the unit became the third squadron of MAG-11 at El Toro. A small skull and two lightning flashes are carried on the fin of the squadron's aircraft, unlike the large and full coloured variant which is painted on the squadron hangar at El Toro.

Below: A VMFA-531 Hornet on the taxiway at El Toro. In the background is the noticeable layer of smog over nearby Los Angeles.

Opposite: The undercarriage is starting to retract as this VMFA-531F/A-18A takes off from its El Toro base.

Below: Photographed off the coast of California is an F/A-18A of VMFA-531 'Grey Ghosts' in company with a CF-18A of 410 'Cougar' Squadron. *(Frank B. Mormillo)*

Below and opposite: A pair of 'Grey Ghosts' Hornets climbing out of El Toro in close formation.

UNITED STATES NAVY

The Navy procured the F/A-18 primarily to replace the A-7 Corsair in the carrier-borne ground attack role. It currently has twenty-one squadrons of Hornets at three locations, with a further six squadrons still to convert. Units serving with the Atlantic Fleet are shore based at NAS Cecil Field, Florida, and those with the Pacific Fleet at NAS Lemoore, California. A further three units which serve aboard the USS *Midway* — the only carrier based outside the US — are shore based at NAS Atsugi, Japan. There are two training squadrons — known as Fleet Replacement Squadrons (FRSs), VFA-106 at Cecil Field and VFA-125 at Lemoore.

The F/A-18C is the variant currently in production for the Navy, and those units with the F/A-18A are slowly converting to the newer model.

The Navy's aerobatic display team, the 'Blue Angels,' are equipped with the F/A-18A.

Opposite: One of the Blue Angels' colourful F/A-18As. The unit also has two F/A-18B two seaters on strength which are, supposedly, used to give orientation flights to members of the press.

Below: Based at Pensacola the Blue Angels spend most of the year travelling throughout the United States attending air shows at both military and civil locations. The aircraft on strength are all early build machines from the first production batch, which are believed to have modifications to the flight control software which make it easier to fly aerobatic manoeuvres. Lined up on the ramp at Andrews AFB, the team are about to depart to give a display at the nearby Naval Academy at Annapolis.

Opposite: Tail markings of VFA-15 'Valions' USN.

Below: The second operational Navy unit to form was VFA-25 'Fist of the Fleet,' which did so in July 1983. Upon conversion to the F/A-18A the unit embarked on the USS *Constellation* with sister unit VFA-113. The squadron has recently upgraded to the F/A-18C, and with the air wing, CVW-14, transferred to the USS *Independence*. One of the squadron's early A model Hornets is illustrated on the ramp at Davis-Monthan AFB. *(GB Aircraft Slides)*

Below: Former A-7E unit VA-15 became VFA-15 on 1 October 1986 with conversion to the F/A-18A. The squadron joined sister unit VFA-87 in CVW-8 and embarked on the USS *Theodore Roosevelt*. With the squadron nickname 'Valions' on the drop tanks, this aircraft was photographed during a visit to RAF Abingdon.

Opposite: VFA-81 'Sunliners' converted from the A-7E to the F/A-18C in February 1988 and assigned to CVW-17 aboard the USS *Saratoga*. A number of Cecil Field based squadrons have now painted full colour unit markings on the aircraft assigned to either the squadron commander or the CAG, as seen on the fin of this aircraft. The air wing code letters 'AA' have been repositioned on the inside of the fin. At the time of writing the squadron is serving aboard the *Saratoga* in the Gulf.

Right: Tail markings of VFA-81 'Sunliners' USN.

Below: This C model Hornet of VFA-81 is probably assigned to the CAG of CVW-17, as the air wing badge has replaced the squadron markings.

Opposite: An F/A-18C of VFA-82 'Marauders' taxies clear of the runway at NAS Cecil Field. This former A-7E Corsair unit converted to the Hornet in July 1987, and is currently serving with the CVW-1 aboard the USS *America*.

Below right: Tail markings of VFA-82 'Marauders' USN.

Below left: Tail markings of VFA-83 'Rampager' USN.

Below: Since 1986 VFA-106 has had the amazing record of a 100 per cent pass rate on pilot qualification, including the demanding carrier qualification phase. An F/A-18C of VFA-106 taxies out for yet another training mission from Cecil.

Opposite: A well-known former A-7 unit which converted to the F/A-18C in July 1987 is VFA-86 'Sidewinders.' This Cecil based unit is assigned to CVW-1 aboard the USS *America* and, like many units, carries the air wing code letters on the inside of the fins. Illustrated is the squadron commander's aircraft, modex '400,' with a full colour Sidewinder snake insignia on the fin.

Opposite: As an A-7 unit VA-87 'Golden Warriors' had one of
the most colourful squadron markings around. However, since its
transition in May 1986 to VFA-87 with F/A-18As these markings
have been somewhat subdued, and now depict a monochrome
Indian chief's head. One of the squadron's aircraft is featured
taxiing past a crowded Cecil Field ramp which still includes a
number of A-7E Corsairs.

Below right: Close-up of CVW-17 badge on the fin of F/A-18C of
VFA-81.

Below left: Tail markings of VFA-86 ' Sidewinders' USN.

Opposite: The task of training pilots for the Navy's east coast units belongs to VFA-106 'Gladiators' at Cecil Field. The squadron disbanded as an operational A-7 unit in 1969, two years after it lost half its aircraft in a disastrous fire aboard the USS *Forrestal*. It reformed again in its present guise on 27 April 1984. Three Hornets of VFA-106 are here seen in company with a pair of A-7E Corsairs from VFA-174, the Corsair training unit which at the time was also based at Cecil Field. *(Don Spering)*

Below: VFA-113 'Stingers' became the first operational Navy squadron to receive the Hornet when it began conversion from the A-7E on 29 March 1983. With sister unit VFA-25, it carried out the Hornet's sea-going début aboard the USS *Constellation* in 1985. It has remained a component of CVW-14 ever since, and upgraded to the F/A-18C in late 1989. Illustrated is one of the squadron's early build A models. *(Frank B. Mormillo)*

Opposite: Tail markings of VFA-106 'Gladiators' USN.

Below: An F/A-18D model of VFA-106 taxies past Royal
Navy Sea Harriers at Cecil Field. This particular aircraft has full
colour unit markings applied.

Opposite: VFA-125 aircraft are devoid of unit markings and carry only the squadron's 'NJ' tailcode on the fin. An F/A-18A taxies past Lemoore's control tower which itself is bedecked with the squadron badges of all resident units. *(Tony Holmes)*

Right: Tail markings of VFA-113 'Stingers' USN.

Below: Photographed on board the USS *Dwight D. Eisenhower* during a visit to British waters is an F/A-18A of VFA-131 which has the squadron nickname emblazoned on the drop tanks. The *Eisenhower* was the first carrier to be employed on Operation Desert Shield duties when the Iraqi forces invaded Kuwait, but has since been relieved by the USS *Saratoga*.

Opposite: VFA-131 'Wildcats' was formed as a Hornet unit at Lemoore in October 1983, and moved to Cecil Field in 1985. The unit was previously known as VF-131 'Nightcappers' which flew the F3H-2 Demon until disestablished in 1962. The 'Wildcats' maiden cruise with CVW-13 aboard the USS *Coral Sea* was with fellow Hornet operators VFA-132, VMFA-314 and VMFA-323. The Hornet's combat début was in March 1986. During Operation Prairie Fire Hornets attacked SAM sites in Libya, and again on 14 April 1986 during Operation El Dorado Canyon, struck specified targets near Benghazi. VFA-131 has since been reassigned to CVW-7 and the USS *Dwight D. Eisenhower*, and is currently converting to the F/A-18C. Illustrated is an A model Hornet while the squadron was serving aboard the USS *Coral Sea*.
(Author's collection)

Below: Tail markings of VFA-131 'Wildcats' USN.

Opposite: Newly reformed at Lemoore in January 1984, VFA-132 'Privateers' transferred to Cecil Field and embarked on the USS *Coral Sea* with CVW-13. During that eventful cruise the squadron's aircraft came under extensive fire from SAMs as they attacked targets in Benghazi. A row of F/A-18As of VFA-131 are seen on the ramp at Cecil Field.

Below: The distinction of being the first Hornet squadron in the world falls to VFA-125 'Rough Raiders,' which formed on 13 November 1980 at Lemoore. The unit was initially responsible for training all pilots destined to fly the F/A-18, be they Navy, Marine or for an export customer. However, now that the additional training units VFA-106 and VMFAT-101 have formed, the 'Rough Raiders' now primarily train pilots for west coast squadrons. An early build two seat Hornet is illustrated during a visit to CFB Cold Lake. At the time the two seat Hornet was designated TF/A-18A; however, this was soon changed to F/A-18B to reflect the trainer variant's combat capability. *(Peter Foster)*

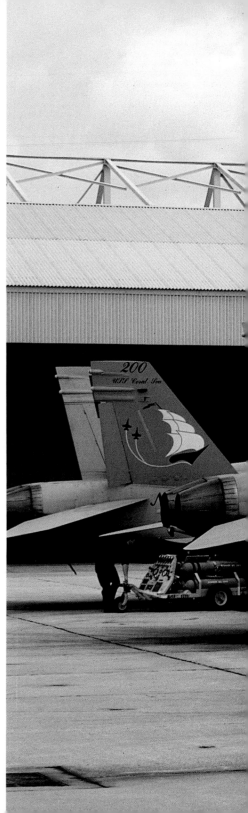

Below: Currently converting to the C model, VFA-136 'Knighthawks' was formed with F/A-18As at Lemoore in July 1985, and soon moved to take up residence at Cecil Field in March 1985. The squadron's first cruise was with CVW-13 on the USS *Coral Sea*; it has since transferred to CVW-7 aboard the USS *Dwight D. Eisenhower*, where this shot was taken.

Opposite: When first formed, VFA-132's tail marking was the head of a pirate. This has now been changed and it features a sailing ship with black sails and the silhouette of two F/A-18s. On the squadron commander's aircraft the sails of the sailing ship are painted white. The unit is unique in that all markings painted on the aircraft are in 'ye olde' style.

Below: Tail markings of VFA-136 'Knighthawks' USN.

Opposite: Newly formed at Cecil Field on 2 July 1985, VFA-137 'Kestrels' has remained a component of CVW-13 aboard the USS *Coral Sea*. Photographed over a towering cloud and in loose formation with a pair of A-6 Intruders is an F/A-18A of VFA-137. *(Author's collection)*

Right: Tail markings of VFA-137 'Kestrels' USN.

Below: One of the most recent units to have disposed of its A-7Es is VA-147, which became VFA-147 'Jasons' and received its first F/A-18Cs in late 1989. This Lemoore based squadron is assigned to CVW-9 aboard the USS *Nimitz*. Photographed on approach to Miramar is the Hornet of VFA-147 assigned to the CAG. *(Andy Thomson)*

Opposite: VFA-151 'Vigilantes' is unique amongst Navy Hornet units as it operated the F-4N Phantom prior to receiving its F/A-18As in June 1986. VFA-161 was also a former Phantom unit; however it was disbanded within two years of forming due to financial cuts which disestablished the air wing it was destined to join. VFA-151 is one of three Hornet squadrons with CVW-5 aboard the USS *Midway*, and was photographed on final approach to its Atsugi base *(Toshiki Kudo)*

Below: Due to its size the USS *Midway*, like the *Coral Sea*, cannot operate the F-14 Tomcat and presently operates three Hornet squadrons which provide both air defence and attack roles. For the latter they are assisted by a pair of A-6E Intruder squadrons. Based at Yokosuka in Japan, the *Midway* is the only carrier based outside the USA. VFA-192 'World Famous Golden Dragons' is one of the three Hornet units assigned, and formed at Lemoore in late 1985 before moving to Atsugi, where this F/A-18A was photographed. *(Toshiki Kudo)*

Below: Taxiing for take-off at its Atsugi base is an F/A-18A of VFA-195 'Dambusters.' This former A-7E squadron formed at Lemoore in April 1985 before moving to its present home in November 1986. The USS *Midway* is due to be retired in 1991 and replaced in Japan by the USS *Independence*. When that happens CVW-5 may receive two F-14 squadrons, and perhaps lose one of its Hornet units. *(Toshiki Kudo)*

UNITED STATES NAVAL RESERVE

Like its air force counterpart, the Naval Reserve often operates modern equipment and presently has three squadrons of F/A-18As with a fourth due to convert during 1991. All previously operated the A-7 Corsair. Two reserve squadrons, VFA-303 and 305, have just completed a short cruise with CVW-11 on the USS *George Washington* as it sailed from Norfolk, Virginia to its new home port of Alameda, California.

Below: VFA-303 'Golden Hawks' was an early recipient of the Hornet. This former Alameda based A-7 unit received its first F/A-18As at Lemoore in 1985, and has remained at Lemoore as a component of CVWR-30. With a stylized 'ND' tailcode superimposed on the Hawk logo, this Hornet was photographed at its Lemoore base. *(Tony Holmes)*

Below: Tail markings of VFA-203 'Blue Dolphins' USNR.

Below: On the range at NAS Fallon a VFA-305 Hornet fires a salvo of Zuni rockets. *(Pat O'Rourke/Frank B. Mormillo)*

Opposite: Based at Cecil Field, VFA-203 'Blue Dolphins' activated as a Hornet unit on 1 October 1989 and is a component of Reserve Carrier Air Wing Twenty (CVWR-20). Some of the squadron's F/A-18As have been handed down from VFA-113, which has now converted to the F/A-18C. This 'Blue Dolphins' aircraft was photographed on the flight line at Cecil in May 1990.

Below: The second west coast reserve Hornet unit is VFA-305
'Lobos' which is based at Point Mugu, California. It disposed of its
A-7 Corsairs and received its first F/A-18As in January 1987.
Photographed over the Pacific is a VFA-305 Hornet in company
with one from VFA-303, its sister unit within CVWR-30.
(Frank B. Mormillo)

Opposite: The unmistakable shape of the Hornet. An early
build F/A-18A of VFA-305 'Lobos' photographed over the Pacific
Ocean off the coast of southern California. *(Frank B. Mormillo)*

AUSTRALIA

The Royal Australian Air Force selected the Hornet to replace its fleet of ageing Mirage IIIs, and fifty-seven single and eighteen two seaters were procured. The first unit to equip was quite naturally the conversion unit, No. 2 Operational Conversion Unit at Williamtown, New South Wales. The first operational squadron, No. 3 was formed at Williamtown on 1 April 1986, the day after it disbanded as a Mirage unit at Butterworth, Malaysia. No. 3 Squadron is primarily an air defence unit with a secondary air to ground role, the ratio being split 60:40. Next to equip with the Hornet, also at Williamtown, was No. 77 Squadron which formed on 1 July 1987. It was previously the Mirage training unit, and is now employed in the air to ground role, with air defence as a secondary task. Again the role is split 60:40. The final unit to convert, and the only one not based at Williamtown, is No. 75 Squadron. It used to operate the Mirage from Darwin until May 1988 when it joined the Hornet club. A few months later the squadron relocated to the newly refurbished base at Tindal in the remote Northern Territories. The squadron has a dual air – air and air – ground role, split 50:50. The unit's flexibility will be significantly enhanced when the RAAF receives its two Boeing 707 tankers. Although the RAAF no longer has a permanent fighter presence at Butterworth, about twice a year Hornets are deployed to the Malaysian base, usually coinciding with a major exercise in the region.

Opposite: A pair of 3 Squadron Hornets low over the coastline of New South Wales. *(RAAF Williamtown)*

Right: A pair of 3 Squadron aircraft in a near vertical climb in the clear blue Aussie skies. Note the toned-down unit badge on the upper fuselage whilst five stars are displayed on the fin. *(RAAF Williamtown)*

Opposite: An F/A-18A of 77 Squadron over Sydney, with the Opera House and Harbour Bridge providing a spectacular background. *(RAAF Williamtown)*

Below right: Tail markings of 2 OCU RAAF.

Below left: A four-ship of Hornets from No. 2 OCU high over New South Wales on a training sortie from their Williamtown base. *(RAAF Williamtown)*

Opposite: At rest underneath the 'bicycle sheds' at Williamtown is 77 Squadron F/A-18B A21-114. The 'bicycle sheds' were built to provide shelter for aircraft and groundcrews during the hot Australian summers, though during my visit they were welcome shelter from the torrential rain! Note the toned-down unit badge and cheatline on the fuselage and speedbird logo on the fin.

Below right: 'Speedbird' logo carried on the fins of 77 Squadron aircraft.

Below left: One of the few single seaters on the strength of the OCU taxies for take-off at Williamtown.

CANADA

The first and largest export order of the F-18 Hornet to date was for the Canadian Armed Forces, in which service it has the official designation CF-188, although this is frequently abbreviated to CF-18. As proof of the Hornet's multi-role capability it was chosen to replace three types in the Canadian Forces; the CF-5 Freedom Fighter, CF-101 Voodoo and CF-104 Starfighter. Initially 113 single seaters and twenty-five two seaters were ordered, but ultimately ninety-eight and forty respectively were delivered.

The first aircraft delivered went to the AETE, followed by twenty or so aircraft to No. 410 Operational Training Squadron at Cold Lake. That unit, known as the 'Cougars,' was activated at Cold Lake in June 1982 and was formerly the Voodoo training unit at Bagotville. The first operational unit was the former Comox based, Voodoo equipped 409 'Nighthawks' Squadron, and was activated at Cold Lake in August 1984. It was planned that 409 would remain at Cold Lake, however fatique problems to the Hornet tail had caused the whole Canadian re-equipment programme to slip. As the CF-104s were being withdrawn from Europe replacements were urgently needed, hence 409 was transferred to the 1st Canadian Air Group at Baden-Sollingen in Germany in June 1985. The next unit to form was another ex-Voodoo unit, No. 425 'Alouette' Squadron at Bagotville in April 1985. Former Starfighter squadrons Nos. 439 'Tiger' and 421 'Red Indian' were next in December 1985 and June 1986, both of which returned to their home base at Sollingen after conversion. The three remaining squadrons are all Canadian based, with ex-CF-104 unit 441 'Silver Fox' Squadron forming at its new base, Cold Lake, in July 1987. In December 1987 the only CF-5 unit to convert to the Hornet was formed; this was No. 433 'Porcupine' Squadron at Bagotville. The remaining unit, No. 416 'Lynx' Squadron, formed in December 1988 and is based at Cold Lake. It was formerly a Voodoo unit at Chatham.

Opposite: Rolling inverted to commence a simulated attack is a CF-18A of 409 'Nighthawk' Squadron. All CAF Hornets have the dummy cockpit painted on the underside which helps to confuse an enemy in air to air combat.

Below: Canada's Aerospace Engineering Test Establishment (AETE) is based at Cold Lake and operates a variety of aircraft types to undertake tests of all aircraft and weapons in the CAF inventory. All AETE aircraft carry a red 'X' denoting 'experimental' on the top fin, as seen on this CF-18B on the runway at Cold Lake. Note the cameras on the wing tip pylons for photographing the release of weapons from the inboard pylons.

Opposite: AETE currently has two single and one two seat Hornets on strength. The latter is seen here banking for its run-in to the Primrose Lake Range near to Cold Lake *(AETE)*

Below: 409 Squadron CF-18A 188752 over southern Germany during a crisp clear winter day. Note that the unit insignia has been reduced in size compared to that worn when the squadron was at Cold Lake.

Opposite: A recent modification designed to ease fatigue on the tail fins is the leading edge extension (LERX) fence on the upper surface of the wing root. As seen in this photograph 410 Squadron have painted their leaping cougar on the fence.

Opposite: A 410 'Cougar' Squadron CF-18 approaches the holding point of runway 30R at Cold Lake. On the port outboard pylon an SUU-20 training weapons dispenser is carried; this is capable of holding six practice bombs and four 2.75in rockets.

Below right: Insignia of 409 'Nighthawk' Squadron CAF.

Below left: Tail markings of 410 'Cougar' Squadron CAF.

Below: No. 1 Canadian Air Group was in 1988 redesignated the 1st Canadian Air Division, with headquarters at Lahr. Component squadrons are 409, 421 and 439 at Baden-Sollingen, however in time of crisis these would be reinforced by 416 Squadron at Cold Lake and 433 Squadron at Bagotville. Illustrated is a CF-18A of 409 Squadron over the unit's 'play area' — Bavaria.

Opposite: The final Sollingen based squadron to equip with the CF-18 was 421 'Red Indian' Squadron, which formed in June 1986. One of the unit's aircraft is seen on take-off from its German base.

Opposite: This 421 Squadron machine was photographed demonstrating the Hornet's capabilities during the 1990 Farnborough Air Show.

Below: A 421 'Red Indian' squadron CF-18A descending at low level over a snowbound southern Germany. The squadron previously operated the CF-104 Starfighter from Sollingen. *(Peter Foster)*

Below: All three Sollingen based squadrons are employed primarily in the air – ground role and as such are assigned to NATO's 4th Allied Tactical Air Force which is headquartered at Ramstein. 421 Squadron CF-18A 188728 was photographed at its Sollingen base during the biennial NATO Tactical Weapons Meet.

Opposite: Seen on take-off at the annual Molson London International Air Show (Ontario) is a 425 Squadron CF-18A. The unit has appeared at this event many times, and the performances of its previous type, the CF-101 Voodoo, are fondly remembered by many.

Opposite: This 416 Squadron CF-18A, aircraft 188798, was the final CAF Hornet to be delivered. In time of war the unit would deploy with Bagotville's 433 Squadron to the 1st Canadian Air Division at Lahr.

Below right: Tail markings of 416 'Lynx' Squadron CAF.

Below left: Tail markings of 421 'Red Indian' Squadron CAF.

Opposite: Sharing Bagotville with 425 Squadron is the other French-speaking CAF unit, No. 433 'Porcupine' Squadron — or, as it prefers to be known, 433 Escadron Tactique de Chasse. This former CF-5 unit converted to the CF-18 in December 1987 and is employed primarily in the air to ground role. The squadron also has a NATO reinforcement role and in company with 416 Squadron can be assigned to the 1st Canadian Air Division at Lahr. This 433 Squadron aircraft was photographed at the Molson London International Air Show (Ontario), and has 425 Squadron markings on the port fin.

Below right: Tail markings of 425 'Alouette' Squadron CAF.

Below left: Tail markings of 433 'Porcupine' Squadron CAF.

Below: Chained down and with intake guards in place, this 433 Squadron aircraft is undergoing full-power engine runs at Cold Lake where the squadron was deployed to participate in a Maple Flag exercise.

Opposite: A 439 'Tiger' Squadron CF-18A in clean configuration seen on climb out. After many years of operating the Starfighter the squadron began conversion to the CF-18 in December 1985.

Opposite: Nestling inside its Hardened Aircraft Shelter (HAS) at its Sollingen base is a 439 'Tiger' Squadron CF-18A.

Below: Tail markings of 439 'Tiger' Squadron CAF.

Below: Like many of the CAF's front line units, No. 441 has a long and proud history, and since it formed in 1942 has operated famous aircraft such as the Hurricane, Spitfire, Mustang, Vampire, Sabre and Starfighter. It disbanded as a Starfighter unit at Sollingen in March 1986. Undergoing systems checks in the units hangar this CF-18A has the luminous formation strips lit. These are a very effective aid to night formation flying.

Opposite: 439 Squadron CF-18A on the Sollingen ramp. Note the thick rope which the Canadians use to chock the aircraft — simple, cheap and very effective. This aircraft, 188742, has larger than normal unit markings on the fin.

Opposite: All Canadian based Hornet units frequently practice air to air refuelling from the CAF's two Boeing CC-137 aircraft which can be equipped as tankers, and the Sollingen based aircraft have also refuelled on occasions from RAF VC-10K tankers. Like all CAF Hornet units, 441 has a small number of two seat CF-18Bs on strength: one of these was photographed taxiing from its parking spot on the Cold Lake flightline.

Below: Tail markings of 441 'Silver Fox' Squadron CAF.

Opposite: Formed in July 1987, No. 441 'Silver Fox' Squadron is based at Cold Lake and tasked with the air defence of western Canada. The unit has aircraft on alert at Comox, British Columbia, but is also tasked with providing cover against attack over the North Pole. For this reason it frequently deploys to FOLs, such as Inuvik, Iqaluit, Rankin Inlet and Yellowknife in the Northwest Territories. Some of these, such as Inuvik, are rather austere locations to say the least, and it is a tremendous achievement that the unit can operate from such locations in the harsh Canadian winters. In this photograph a 441 Squadron aircraft has just intercepted a Soviet Mig-29; however on this occasion the 'bogey' has no hostile intentions, and is being escorted to Abbotsford to participate in the air show. *(441 Squadron)*

Below: A 441 Squadron Hornet fires an AIM-7 Sparrow.
(441 Squadron)

SPAIN

The first of seventy-two EF-18 Hornets for the Spanish Air Force flew on 3 March 1986, and the twelve two seat EF-18Bs were first off the production line. Initial training was conducted in the USA before the aircraft were delivered to Spain with the aid of in-flight refuelling by USAF KC-10 tankers; all aircraft were subsequently delivered by the same method. The first unit to receive the new aircraft was the newly re-formed Ala 15 at Zaragoza, which comprised 151 and 152 Escuadrones. Ala 15 previously operated the F-86 Sabre until that type was withdrawn in the 1970s, and the unit remained dormant until re-forming on 16 December 1985 to prepare for its new machines. Although not worn on the aircraft, Ala 15 adopted the tiger insignia of Grupo 41. Ala 15 was at full strength by mid-1988 when aircraft for Ala 12 began to arrive at Zaragoza where personnel would be trained. Ala 12 and its Escuadrones, 121 and 122, transferred to its Torrejon base in 1989 to replace the F-4C Phantoms. The Spanish Air Force operates a small fleet of KC-130 Hercules tankers from Zaragoza, and the EF-18s are one of their regular customers. Although Spanish Hornets carry unit code letter on the nose, to date they have been devoid of unit badges.

Opposite: Ala 12 EF-18A C.15-46 coded '12-04' seen at Zaragoza while crews of 121 Escuadron were converting to the type.

Below: A two seat EF-18B of Ala 12 in the early morning Spanish sunshine. Note the small black St. Andrew's cross national marking at the top of the rudder.

Opposite: Both Ala 12 and 15 each have six two seat EF-18Bs; this is CE.15-6 '15-75' from the latter unit.

APPENDIX A
F-18 HORNET OPERATORS

UNITED STATES NAVY

Unit	Code	Model	Unit name	Base
VFA-15	'AJ'	F-18A	Valions	Cecil Field
VFA-22	'NH'	F-18C	Redcocks	Lemoore
VFA-25	'NK'	F-18C	Fist of the Fleet	Lemoore
VFA-27	'NL'	F-18C	Chargers	Lemoore
VFA-81	'AA'	F-18C	Sunliners	Cecil Field
VFA-82	'AB'	F-18C	Marauders	Cecil Field
VFA-83	'AA'	F-18C	Rampagers	Cecil Field
VFA-86	'AB'	F-18C	Sidewinders	Cecil Field
VFA-87	'AJ'	F-18A	Golden Warriors	Cecil Field
VFA-94	'NH'	F-18C	Mighty Shrikes	Lemoore
VFA-97	'NL'	F-18C	Warhawks	Lemoore
VFA-105	'AE'	F-18A	Gunslingers	Cecil Field
VFA-106	'AD'	F-18A-D	Gladiators	Cecil Field
VFA-113	'NK'	F-18C	Stingers	Lemoore
VFA-125	'NJ'	F-18A-D	Rough Raiders	Lemoore
VFA-131	'AG'	F-18C	Wildcats	Cecil Field
VFA-132	'AK'	F-18A	Privateers	Cecil Field
VFA-136	'AG'	F-18C	Knighthawks	Cecil Field
VFA-137	'AK'	F-18A	Kestrels	Cecil Field
VFA-146	'NG'	F-18C	Blue Diamonds	Lemoore
VFA-147	'NG'	F-18C	Jasons	Lemoore
VFA-151	'NF'	F-18A	Vigilantes	Atsugi
(VFA-161)		(F-18A)	Chargers Disbanded 1 April 1988	Lemoore —
VFA-192	'NF'	F-18A	World Famous Golden Dragons	Atsugi
VFA-195	'NF'	F-18A	Dambusters	Atsugi

Planned to form:

Unit		Model	Unit name	Base
VFA-37		F-18A	Bulls	Cecil Field
VFA-46		F-18C	Clansmen	Cecil Field
VFA-56		F-18C	Champions	Lemoore
VFA-72		F-18C	Bluehawks	Cecil Field
VFA-93		F-18C	Ravens	Lemoore

Carrier assignments:

CVW-17	'AA'	USS *Saratoga*
CVW-1	'AB'	USS *America*
CVW-5	'AE'	USS *Forrestal*
CVW-7	'AG'	USS *Dwight D Eisenhower*
CVW-8	'AJ'	USS *Theodore Roosevelt*
CVW-13	'AK'	USS *Coral Sea*
CVW-5	'NF'	USS *Midway*
CVW-9	'NG'	USS *Nimitz*
CVW-11	'NH'	USS *Abraham Lincoln*
CVW-14	'NK'	USS *Independence*
CVW-15	'NL'	USS *Carl Vinson*

UNITED STATES NAVAL RESERVE

Unit	Code	Model	Unit name	Base
VFA-203	'AF'	F-18A	Blue Dolphins	Cecil Field
VFA-303	'ND'	F-18A	Golden Hawks	Lemoore
VFA-305	'ND'	F-18A	Lobos	Point Mugu

Planned to form:

Unit	Code	Model	Unit name	Base
VFA-204	'AF'	F-18A	River Rattlers	New Orleans

MISCELLANEOUS UNITS

	Code	Model	Unit name	Base
Blue Angels		F-18A		Pensacola
VX-4	'XF'	F-18A/C/D	Evaluators	Point Mugu
VX-5	'XE'	F-18A	Vampires	China Lake
NSWC		F-18A/B	Naval Strike Warfare Center	Fallon
NWC		F-18A/D	Naval Weapons Center	China Lake
PMTC		F-18A/B/C	Pacific Missile Test Center	Point Mugu
NATC/SATD	'SD'	F-18A/C/D	Naval Air Test Center Strike Aircraft Test Directorate	Patuxent River
NATC/NTPS		F-18B	Naval Air Test Center Test Pilot School	Patuxent River
NASA		F-18A/B	National Aeronautics & Space Administration	Edwards

UNITED STATES MARINE CORPS

Unit	Code	Model	Unit name	Base
VMFAT-101	'SH'	F-18A-D	Sharpshooters	El Toro
VMFA-115	'VE'	F-18A	Silver Eagles	Beaufort
VMFA(AW)-121	'VK'	F-18D	Green Knights	El Toro
VMFA-122	'DC'	F-18A	Crusaders	Beaufort
VMFA-212	'WD'	F-18C	Lancers	Kaneohe Bay
VMFA-232	'WT'	F-18C	Red Devils	Kaneohe Bay
VMFA-235	'DB'	F-18C	Death Angels	Kaneohe Bay
VMFA-251	'DW'	F-18A	Thunderbolts	Beaufort
VMFA-312	'DR'	F-18A	Checkertails	Beaufort
VMFA-314	'VW'	F-18A	Black Knights	El Toro
VMFA-323	'WS'	F-18A	Death Rattlers	El Toro
VMFA-333	'DN'	F-18A	Shamrocks	Beaufort
VMFA-451	'VM'	F-18A	Warlords	Beaufort
VMFA-531	'EC'	F-18A	Grey Ghosts	El Toro

Planned to form:

Unit	Code	Model	Unit name	Base
VMFA(AW)-224	'WK'	F-18D	Bengals	Cherry Point
VMFA(AW)-225	'CE'	F-18D	Vagabonds	El Toro
VMFA(AW)-242	'DT'	F-18D	Batmen	El Toro
VMFA(AW)-332	'EA'	F-18D	Moonlighters	Cherry Point
VMFA(AW)-533	'ED'	F-18D	Hawks	Cherry Point

UNITED STATES MARINE CORPS RESERVE

Unit	Code	Model	Unit name	Base
VMFA-134	'MF'	F-18A	Hawks	El Toro

Planned to form:

Unit	Code	Model	Unit name	Base
VMFA-112	'MA'	F-18A	Cowboys	Dallas
VMFA-321	'MG'	F-18A	Hell's Angels	Andrews

ROYAL AUSTRALIAN AIR FORCE

Unit	Model	Unit name	Base
2 OCU	F-18A/B		Williamtown
3 Squadron	F-18A		Williamtown
75 Squadron	F-18A		Tindal
77 Squadron	F-18A		Williamtown

CANADIAN ARMED FORCES

Unit	Model	Unit name	Base
AETE	CF-18A/B		Cold Lake
409 Squadron	CF-18A	Night Hawks	Sollingen
410 Squadron	CF-18A/B	Cougars	Cold Lake
416 Squadron	CF-18A	Lynx	Cold Lake
421 Squadron	CF-18A	Red Indians	Sollingen
425 Squadron	CF-18A	Alouettes	Bagotville
433 Squadron	CF-18A	Porcupines	Bagotville
439 Squadron	CF-18A	Sabre Tooth Tigers	Sollingen
441 Squadron	CF-18A	Silver Foxes	Cold Lake

SPANISH AIR FORCE

Unit	Model	Base
Ala 12		
121 Escuadron	EF-18A	Torrejon
122 Escuadron	EF-18A	Torrejon
Ala 15		
151 Escuadron	EF-18A	Zaragoza
152 Escuadron	EF-18A	Zaragoza

Note: all Australian, Canadian and Spanish operational squadrons operate a few two seat B models.

APPENDIX B
PRODUCTION LIST

USN/USMC:

No. in batch	Serial Number	Model	
(2)	160775 — 160776	YF-18A	
(9)	160777 — 160785	F-18A/B	(B; 781)
(5)	161213 — 161217	F-18A/B	(B; 217)
(4)	161248 — 161251	F-18A/B	(B; 249)
(15)	161353 — 161367	F-18A/B	(B; 354 – 357, 360)
(10)	161519 — 161528	F-18A	
(60)	161702 — 161761	F-18A/B	(B; 704, 707, 711, 714, 719, 723, 727, 733, 740, 746)
(64)	161924 — 161987	F-18A/B	(B; 924, 932, 938, 943, 947)
(84)	162394 — 162477	F-18A/B	(B; 402, 408, 413, 419, 427)
(84)	162826 — 162909	F-18A/B	(B; 836, 842, 850, 857, 870, 876, 885)*
(84)	163092 — 163175	F-18A/B	(B; 104, 110)*
(84)	163427 — 163510	F-18C/D	(D; 434, 441, 445, 452, 454, 457, 472, 474, 482, 486, 488, 492, 500, 501, 507, 510)*
(84)	163699 — 163782	F-18C/D	(D; 700, 707, 718, 720, 734, 740, 749, 763, 771, 778)
(84)	163985 — 164068	F-18C/D	(D; 986, 989, 991, 994, 997, 001, 005, 009, 011, 014, 017, 019, 022, 024, 026, 028, 032, 035, 038, 040, 043, 046, 049, 051, 053, 056, 058, 061, 064, 068)
(126)	164196 — 164321	F-18C/D	(D; 196, 198)*
	(164332 — 164339)	F-18C/D	[CANCELLED ORDER]
	(164411 — 164422)	F-18C	[CANCELLED ORDER]

* batch details for B/D models not complete

RAAF

(57)	A21-1 — A21-57	F/A-18A	
(18)	A21-101 — A21-118	F/A-18B	
(75)			

CAF

(98)	188701 — 188798	CF-18A	
(40)	188901 — 188940	CF-18B	
(138)			

SPANISH AF

(12)	CE15-1 — CE15-12	EF-18B	
(60)	C15-13 — C15-72	EF-18A	
(72)			